U BECOME BLOOD

Triumph Through Pain

A Devotional Towards Love Into the Bridal Chamber.

DIANNA HENDERSON

DEDICATION

I dedicate this book to the Bride, the "Church," and all who choose not to live in pain. But rather to live and experience a life of freedom from blood tears.

"Jesus said, it is finished."

(John 19:30)

TESTIMONIALS

From birth we are hurled from the sanctity of the womb into a wild world. Mired in chaos, confusion, and the evil that has so dominated the human condition. When it comes to suffering, illness, loss, pain, injustice and trials, none are exempt.

The Book of Job wrestles openly and honestly with the fundamental issues of suffering, raising more questions than it has answers. Yet, in this life faith is truly the victory that overcomes the world (1 John 5:4). Time and again, so many of the Bible's great heroes of faith embraced trials and afflictions as prime learning experiences.

"When Tears Become Blood, Triumph Through Pain" is written by a sufferer to sufferers. Having known Dianna Henderson and her late husband, Bishop William Henderson; I have seen first-hand how they braved the many heartaches and disappointments life threw at them. This was a couple united by a common vision to restore and resurrect a treasured Buffalo historical landmark and to bring spiritual rebirth to the hurting of the community.

The book you now hold in your hands is sure to bring comfort, solace, and encouragement, it comes from the heart of one who's learned from experience that the

Lord is good and His mercy endures forever! May the Great Physician bring healing, restoration, and strength to all who are hungry to hear from Him.

Rabbi Frank Lowinger
Congregation Brith Hadoshah

Pain is a threshold that we have all experienced at one time or another; some more so than others. Living in this world today exposes us to a myriad of traumatic experiences that occur at the most inopportune times. But through those traumatic times of monumental magnitude in my life my tears became blood due to the severity of the pain and unending pressures. Through this I found my place of refuge enabling me to triumph through my trauma. Showing me a pathway of escape to walk triumphantly through, past, over and above my tears of blood to an

abundant victorious life in Crist Jesus. This book displays encouragement and love of how to triumph through pain and I truly can identify with the message of this book. Life is not a bed of roses. Roses have beauty and sweet fragrance, but the sharp thorns will surely pierce the skin bringing forth blood.

Bishop Herman White Jr.
Chair of the Board, Light Of The World Missions, Inc.

"When continued traumatic events and pain are mixed together," writes the author, it becomes like a shedding of blood tears seen through the eyes of complex trauma." This book points the way to this "TRIUMPH" through faith in God, as we experience and embrace the heartbeat of our Father's love. In doing so, we may conquer such things as lack of care, disappointment, depression, loneliness, and grief in all of its expressions. As a result, the reader will be strengthened in personal faith and enabled to help others meet the various crises of life.

Apostle William A. Dockery
Sr. Pastor, Memorial Temple Christian Ministries & Chief Apostle, Covenant Ministries International

We learn character because character is revealed in Jesus Christ. Gaining character comes through genuine love which is a process of pain. Our response to each trial must include thanking God for all things He has done, rejoicing in all things and learning to cry out to God. Dianna has been refined through fiery trials and she has learned to overcome all obstacles. She truly is God's amazing woman.

Pastor Donna Naedele
Pastor of My Father's House Ministries

From the furnace of affliction, God has remarkably chosen Dianna Henderson to transpose supernatural resiliency into a life changing script. Dianna's courage, grace, and poise - in the face of horrendous trials - leaves us this priceless gift for extracting powerful examples to emulate. This book eloquently lifts the reader from the quicksand-like pull of trauma, to the resurrection power and life of Triumph.

Elder Victor Bagnato
Founder of Collateral Hope & Recovery

When the title of this book was revealed to me, I immediately began to study my hands. I thought about creation and the blood; the sweat and tears that come with forming something from nothing. In order to create, one must be inspired. Sometimes this inspiration comes when you least expect it. Sometimes it doesn't show up at all. But when it is a constant, magical ideas, great feats, and unlikely events can occur.

My mother, Dianna Henderson's, inspiration is deep and comes from a place of love, faith, understanding, and forgiveness. These principles are the bedrock of who she is. She is the true embodiment of Pablo Picasso's quote, "The meaning of life is to find your gift. The purpose of life is to give it away." To me, her gift is her being an inspiration to other people, through her openness and willingness to share her life, through all of its ups and downs. This book is a new exploration and use of her gift as she shares her wisdom and words with the world.

I am constantly amazed by my mother, Dianna Henderson. She is my inspiration. Every day she works to become a better version of herself. Even though she is already perfect in my eyes, it is truly a blessing for me to watch her in action, using her gifts to uplift others.

Addison Henderson
CEO, Night Owl Republic, Son to Dianna Henderson

As a young person who has experienced collective traumatic events in The United States such as 9-11/the collapse of the Twin Towers, countless fatalities due to mass shootings, and the loss of community members due to white supremacy, it has altered my life dramatically, changing who I am, and often leaving me to question my true purpose. Reading, *When Tears Become Blood, Triumph Through Pain* became a moment of therapy for me! Guiding me into a meditative space where I could allow my inward wounds to be healed and my tears to be wiped away. As a reader you will continually feel connected to the words and the spiritual revival that Dianna Henderson so eloquently brings to the page.

Rachel Henderson
Actress, writer & daughter to Dianna Henderson

The sun rises before us and the sun sets after we are gone. We face challenges during that time, this book is a testament of that.

Dwand Stevens

Son to Dianna Henderson

Traumas are negative experiences that we have endured in our lives. Whether the experience has been for a few minutes, hours or days, it lingers in our minds and has a profound impact on our reactions, decisions and what we feel about ourselves. Today, you have an open invitation to enter the chamber and surrender your pain so that you can find peace and transform your hurt into healing.

Lorraine Wright,

LCSW "R", *Gatehouse Professional Center*

FOREWORD

When *Tears Become Blood*, is a literal phrase used to describe Jesus as he experienced unimaginable agony while praying, so much so that his sweat became like drops of blood. This is a process that causes hematidrosis, "a condition in which capillary blood vessels that feed the sweat glands rupture, causing them to exude blood; it occurs under conditions of extreme physical or emotional stress." Well, Reverend Dianna Henderson conveys some extraordinary events in her remarkable journey. She encountered physical attacks in her youth from a family friend, was assaulted in the military as a soldier, had a child in her teenage years, and experienced grief and sorrow when she lost the love of her life, Bishop William Henderson. Surely, Reverend Henderson has had moments when her tears became blood from her sorrow, sadness and struggle. I can imagine she felt like Jesus when he came to the threshold of death and said, "my soul is deeply grieved, to the point of death" (Matthew 26:38 NAS). So too her soul must have been disturbed by these encounters.

Nonetheless, this brilliant book does not depict a victim in Reverend Dianna Henderson, but a victorious woman who triumphed through pain and disappointments. Throughout her journey, she cultivated her faith and belief in the sovereign God which caused her to become an overcomer, and victorious in Christ. She rose from the ashes and became an incredible mother, an activist for the underprivileged, an exceptional wife, author, preacher, psalmist, and the list continues. She did not allow her odious life encounters to define her. Together with God, she wrote a new narrative for herself and added a new chapter called, "Victorious."

Let Reverend Diana Henderson's life become a paradigm and an example to emulate during those moments when you are having tears like blood. This book will inspire and encourage its readers allowing them to become triumphant in their journey.

Be Resilient

Rev. Dr. T. Anthony Bronner

Elim Christian Fellowship

God's Peace and Good Journey!

TABLE OF CONTENTS

PREFACE

WHEN TEARS BECOME BLOOD

*He gave me life and unfailing love. My life was
preserved by His care. (Job 10:12)*

I want to share with you that when this book came
into being, it was an act of heroism and a
celebration of the Father's unshakable love.

Painful experiences are different in the lives of
each individual. I personally understand the effects;
which has presented more than a challenge throughout
my life. But I believe God carried me through when I
dwelt with Him in the secret place; shedding my blood
tears and becoming whole in a place of healing.

My personal journey from pain to praise started as a
jubilant youngster. I loved life! I was one who would
play dress up one minute and become a fierce protector
of those I cared about the next. My mother would often
say, "child, you can't be out there fighting people bigger
than you." You see, I was a tiny soul. Everyone in the
neighborhood knew they could call on me and that my
family had their back. In my early teen years, I became

a babysitter for close family and friends. This was such a positive experience for me because I absolutely loved children. Until one day, I was violated; that was my tear.

I encountered a sexual assault. I had no prior knowledge of anything related to this type of behavior. As I was babysitting one evening, the children's uncle came over after they went to sleep. I wasn't alarmed because he was a family friend who we trusted and I was comfortable around him. But I was shocked and startled; as he began to pursue and coerce me to take part in an unwarranted sexual act. It was like he became Dr. Jekyll and Mr. Hyde; whereas, I felt helpless through this encounter of rape and abuse. I was belittled and didn't want him to see my tears of anguish that was pouring out from the wound he was creating within me. This violation continued for months. At first I was appalled, then I hate to admit; it felt good for a moment. But in reality, I was paralyzed in my pain and far removed from the incidents because abuse does that.

Now this was a man my parents trusted; who was around *all* five of their daughters and accepted as family. My parents were known to be very protective of their girls. They would have never imagined their long-time friend would have violated their trust. So it was a very hard and a fearful moment for me when I had to tell my mother. She was simply devastated and my father was furious. But I can honestly say that there was no further mention of his name or sight of him again.

Later as a high school junior, I had a son which caused me to grow up and become more responsible. Thankfully, I had strong support and mentors from my mother and aunt. They gave me the tools to continue pursuing my dreams and hopes. In my twenties, my friend and I unexpectedly signed up for the military. After I passed the exam, I told the recruiter that I couldn't set a date until he first spoke with my mother. It's not that I needed her permission but I wanted her respect. However, she wasn't surprised. She always said that I was different and would go on to excel.

While I was in the military, I decided to attend a birthday celebration for a mutual Drill Sergeant with a few friends. As I was waiting alone, I didn't get the memo but no one showed up. Then he began to come onto me. I became intimidated; too afraid and found myself yet again being sexually assaulted. I was leaving within a month, but I went to see the Army medical physician and shared my experience. He just dismissed me and my complaint; as if it was insignificant and normal behavior. I left feeling robbed, exposed and hopeless. The sum total of my life had begun to feel worthless at the hands of destructive dream killers. But although I was violated, enraged and shattered, I didn't report the incident. However, I did muster up the strength to confront the Drill Sergeant and finally left. Afterwards, this made me withdraw from men and myself. I was losing touch with my emotions; a feeling of disconnect and denying of intimacy. Whereas, I became so unforgiving; I trusted no one. I carried this trauma of mental and emotional torment for years; walking around with fear, unhealthy thoughts and contemplating taking my own life. This was when tears became blood - a prelude to death.

Who knew that what I had gone through would alter my life - changing my joy into devastation, my hope into pain; and living a life of unforgiveness. The agony of my heart was one that eventually shifted over into my marriage of 40 plus years to a wonderful man. It took courage and strength to reach out for support and help through counseling, forgiveness, and moments of raw and emotional release.

Then in 2021, I lost the love of my life and my dearest partner; my safe place. One year later, I was diagnosed with Invasive Ductal Carcinoma Breast Cancer. I had two surgeries, along with chemotherapy, radiation treatment, and immunotherapy. Besides that, my inward wounds of trauma, loss of identity, and grief were all-consuming.

For you made me suffer a lot, but you will bring me back from this deep pit and give me new life (Psalm 71:20 CEV)

As painful as this was, it almost took a lifetime of healing as *I* now *triumph* in *victory*!

There are about 6 out of 10 men and 5 out of every 10 women who will experience at least one traumatic event in their life. Exposure to this type of pain can cause negative side effects; affecting the total well-being of a person for an extended period of time. This includes bullying, community violence, disasters, early childhood trauma, domestic abuse, or even a car accident to name a few. But today as we delve deeper into the Father's love, we can declare to ourselves:

"Enough is Enough! I am Determined to Triumph Through my Pain and into Victory!"

Now take a moment to experience and embrace the heartbeat of the Father. Believe that His love for you surpasses the natural realms of what you feel or know. It travels deep into the essence of your DNA and into the core of your very being. This is not a love that leaves you disappointed or bitter; but better. It is one full of peace, joy, and confidence; that gives you the freedom to relinquish your pain.

Jeremiah 31:3 (KJV) reads,

"The Lord hath appeared of old unto me, saying, Yea, I have loved thee with an everlasting love: therefore, with lovingkindness have I drawn thee,"

Now, travel with me as we take this dimensional journey from abuse to wholeness, from suicide to hope, and from acts of violence to restoration. This will bring you to a place of freedom and remind you that You are More than a Conqueror!

You Are a Warrior in the Midst of Blood Tears

LAMENT

TRIUMPH THROUGH PAIN

Through the triumph of all your tears, acute pain, and complex trauma, **your** voice should rise above the ashes of life. On the wings of hope, the risen Christ rose to make all things new as **you** triumph through pain. We cannot disregard the suffering of humanity; even Christ took on the entirety of our suffering so that we may rise with healing in our being of existence. You may grieve and cry out to God as you move from pain to praise in the Bridal Chamber. Yet, you will triumph through your challenging circumstances!

Psalm 13

A Lament of Reconciliation In Challenging Circumstances

How long, LORD? Will you forget me forever?

How long will you hide your face from me?

How long must I wrestle with my thoughts

and day after day have sorrow in my heart?

How long will my enemy triumph over me?

Look on me and answer, LORD my God.

Give light to my eyes, or I will sleep in death,

and my enemy will say, "I have overcome him,"

and my foes will rejoice when I fall.

But I trust in your unfailing love;

my heart rejoices in your salvation.

I will sing the LORD's praise,

for he has been good to me.

Considering, I will thrive from the ashes of life!

EMERGENCY 911

Your Pain Will Identify Itself

CARRYING YOUR PAIN INTO THE BRIDAL CHAMBER

Throughout life we experience many types of pain, and sometimes that pain can be crippling and traumatizing. Along with pain, trauma can leave us feeling deeply vulnerable and helpless. Trauma is defined as a deeply distressing or a disturbing event. Some examples include the loss of a spouse, a child, a parent, or other family members. Other painful events can include community or domestic violence; disaster, divorce, sexual abuse, a worldwide pandemic, or a life altering accident or illness. The loss of a friendship, upsetting gossip, false accusations, lies, bullying, racism, hateful comments, financial crises, loss of job, and life addictions can all precipitate traumas.

Trauma can come as a direct experience, witnessing someone else's agony, or hearing of someone's pain. Seeking professional support can be helpful. It has helped me to come face-to-face with my own hurt, identifying it, and removing the mask. Once that happened, I was able to embrace the real "Me." Now, this is where I took that daring step and made the decision to no longer remain a prisoner but instead, walk towards my freedom. It was in the Bridal

Chamber, a secret place; that was safe and like no other. This is the place which emanates God's presence, true love, forgiveness, empowerment, confidence, and liberty. Only through His healing and true love, have I learned to love myself after my traumatic events. I carried a dark shadow throughout life and with it came shame, guilt, and hopelessness, even throughout marriage. In the past, it contributed to a counterfeit love; a love in all the wrong places because of what my experiences had taught me. But Jesus demonstrated an authentic love when he paid the price at Calvary. Moreover, being in love with a true lover is like a unified heartbeat. This heartbeat releases the pain of rejection into a heartbeat of acceptance, freedom, peace, and joy.

To become one with the Father; our Heavenly Bridegroom, there must be a willingness of obedience to accept His pure love. The Father desires this unity as He carries your pain into the Bridal Chamber. In the scriptures, Jesus conveys that "I and my Father are one" (John 10:30, KJV). Today, He is offering you an opportunity for healing. Will you accept?

REFLECTIONS

List or identify the type of trauma or pain you are carrying today?

_____

_____

_____

_____

_____

_____

Name what type of support is accessible to you in your community or through your connections (e.g. family, friends, a support group or church)?

_____

_____

_____

_____

_____

_____

What would keep you from stepping out to embrace the true love of Jesus Christ and surrender?

_____

_____

_____

_____

_____

_____

IN THE CHAMBER OF HER WOMB

To better understand the ideal of the Bridal Chamber of the heavenly Bridegroom, let us take a look at the chamber of Mary's womb, which gave birth to the Son of God. Mary, the mother of Jesus, carried the greatest gift and gave birth to the Savior of the world as the *"Son of the Most High,"* (Luke 1:26-38, NRSV).

In the New Testament, Mary was faithful in serving God's prophetic plan as a virgin whose son was not begotten by Joseph (Matthew 1:16). It was during the birthing pains of pregnancy that she surrendered to the call of God by stating, *"Here am I, the servant of the Lord; let it be with me according to Your word"* (Luke 1:38).

There are times when we are carrying pain because we are in a place of birthing a release, naturally or spiritually. In my own experience, pain came unexpectedly while serving four and a half years in the United States Army as an E5 with an honorable discharge; a level for a specialist or a sergeant. I was sexually assaulted during this time and carried the trauma for many years. With the freedom of release, I was able to walk in my long-awaited healing.

Do not abort your pain but carry it to full term and the Bridegroom will carry you to freedom. You will have your moments; where you will be angry, fearful, or crying. You will also experience flashbacks, overwhelming guilt, shame, a loss of faith, depression, trouble sleeping or concentrating; as well as feelings of being alone, helpless or suicidal. Personally, I was blessed to bring forth three beautiful children, naturally and through a cesarean. Also, the Lord gave me the gift of love with a long lasting marriage of over forty years. In addition to Him using me as His servant for His service and sharing the Good News.

The Chamber of God's heart prepares and secures true love with Him. This love can only be found in the Bridal Chamber where peace, healing, forgiveness, and God's everlasting presence abounds.

REFLECTIONS

State why you may find it difficult to release your pain and let it go?

_____

_____

_____

_____

_____

Are you ready to walk in forgiveness with others or yourself and accept God's love?

_____

_____

_____

_____

_____

_____

Describe what forgiveness looks like, what that means to you, and the steps you can take now?

_____

_____

_____

_____

_____

**Aborting your pain does not allow
you freedom to identify it**

You Have Reached Your Destination

Be Liberated in Your Pain to Praise

THE CALL

O ne day as I was driving home, I heard in my spirit, "You are called to the Bridal Chamber." I became quiet and focused within my heart and spirit to receive the message.

My thoughts reflected on Queen Esther's call to the Bridal Chamber; a holy place. She questioned her worthiness about accepting the call (Esther chapters 1-10). She was a member of the Jewish race; who later used her influence as a consort; to fraternize to save her people from extermination through the plot of Haman. Esther was gathered into the king's palace for preparation along with other young women and guarded by Hegai; the custodian. Esther received favor as a servant, and as stated,

"So when the king's order and his edict were proclaimed, and when many young women were gathered in the citadel of Susa in custody of Hegai, Esther also was taken into the king's palace and put in custody of Hegai, who had charge of the women. The girl pleased him and won his favor, and he quickly provided her with her cosmetic treatments and her portion of food, and with seven chosen maids from the king's palace, and advanced her and her maids to the best place in the harem," (Esther 2:8-9).

A call to the Bridal Chamber can be delicate, challenging, painful, questionable, and rewarding. There are many times we may be distracted from responding to the call of God, and this will usually involve uncertainty and skepticism. But what seemed to be a defeat turned out to be a victory in Esther's heart. In this holy place, her transition moved her from loss to hope, from pain to gain, and from victim to victor. Here, she had felt the conviction to reveal the truth about her ethnicity and the plight of her people. Therefore in her perseverance, she went forward and spoke to King Ahasuerus.

Esther's presence in the Bridal Chamber demonstrated God's love, courage, and forgiveness. It was there that she received royal treatment in the inner courts of the king's palace (Esther 5:1-8). A royal banquet was held for his new queen, Queen Esther.

Sometimes through trauma, pain, brokenness and tears of blood, truth can be revealed. It can also release true freedom by freeing others. As Christians, we are called to *liberate* not through restraints, but *love.* Remember, Jesus came to set the captives free.

"The Spirit of the Lord is upon me, because he has anointed me to bring good news to the poor. He has sent me to proclaim release to the captives and recovery of sight to the blind, to let the oppressed go free," (Luke 4:18).

Esther did well with hiding her pain outside the Bridal Chamber; until she was released to step into it. She came face to face with her grief as she presented truth in love to King Ahasuerus and was set free. Yet, just as in Queen Esther's situation, conviction in the Bridal Chamber can produce the freedom to free others, healing wounds for the wounded, hope for the hopeless, and authentic love for the loveless.

REFLECTIONS

What are your biggest reservations or distractions that are keeping you from entering the Bridal Chamber?

_____

_____

_____

_____

_____

_____

List anything you may be hiding that would keep you from moving to a place of freedom?

_____

_____

_____

_____

_____

_____

How do you see yourself helping or interceding for others?

_____

_____

_____

_____

_____

_____

THE ASSIGNMENT

W e have been discussing being called into the Bridal Chamber, but there is more. We must first learn what our assignment or role should be as we enter.

As we are discovering our assignment or call to the Bridal Chamber, it may not be clear until we make a conscious decision to surrender. Even through the darkness of trauma, you the Bride will become liberated and free through the pressure of pain. For we were destined to be called to the Chamber before coming forth from the womb. The Scripture has declared, *"Before I formed you in the womb I knew you, and before you were born, I consecrated you; I appointed you a prophet to the nations,"* (Jeremiah 1:5).

Know that this is the place where you are no longer a tattered victim, but a strong and faithful warrior. Therefore, embrace your assigned purpose and receive God's guidance. The Father never releases a charge without empowering you with resilience and strength to carry it out. He trusts His assignment with those who dare to follow it.

Furthermore, may our Father, the Bridegroom, breathe on you a fresh anointing of love for accepting the call. Considering, the Bridal Chamber compels you to come face-to-face and surrender to your assignment. He is waiting for your response.

REFLECTIONS

What are the obstacles keeping you from making a decision to be free?

_____

_____

_____

_____

_____

Can you see yourself coming face to face with your assigned purpose today?

_____

_____

_____

_____

_____

Take a moment and identify areas in your life where you have been resilient.

_____

_____

_____

_____

_____

**Surrender to the pain and it will free
you on your journey**

Safe and Secure

Do Not Allow the Struggles of Pain to Keep You Captive but Instead Conquer It

THE STRUGGLES

Along with the assignment, there will be struggles in the Bridal Chamber. In life we may struggle because of unknown factors, and we may even question our faith. We might ask questions such as: "Where is this journey going to take me?" "Is it real?" "Will I feel secure in this love?"

Well, in today's America, we are struggling with a high rate of crime, unemployment, food shortage in many families, global sicknesses, loss of loved ones, a high divorce rate, a rapidly declining educational system, a corrupt government and many other painful matters. There are times when it is hard to identify trauma when there are layers. But there is an everlasting love that never fails within the struggles of life. The Lord will carry you and help you triumph through pain as he indicated,

"Come to me, all you that are weary and are carrying heavy burdens, and I will give you rest. Take my yoke upon you and learn from me; for I am gentle and humble in heart, and you will find rest for your souls. For my yoke is easy, and my burden is light," *(Matthew 11:28-30).*

Sometimes love is demonstrated with a fabricated deceit of "untruths." But there is an authentic love in the struggle that can sustain you to the end, and that love is the unconditional love of God. The Bridegroom's love never fails, and He is waiting for your response to join Him in union. He will not leave you in the middle of struggle, pain, or hurt. In fact, He declares His commitment to you:

"I will never leave you or forsake you," (Hebrews 13:5).

The Bridegroom will be by your side and promises His Love. This is His oath and word of honor,

"So you can say with confidence, The Lord is my helper; I will not be afraid. What can anyone do to me?" (Hebrews 13:6).

The Bridegroom is declaring today that you are secured in His heartfelt love, even through trauma and your struggles. Therefore, be at peace!

Reflections

Today, what's keeping you from entering the Bridal Chamber?

_____

_____

_____

_____

_____

_____

What layers of pain and trauma will you have to peel back to face your struggles and move forward?

_____

_____

_____

_____

_____

_____

Take a moment to write down some of His promises that you can apply to your life..

_____

_____

_____

_____

_____

_____

PAIN IN THE CHAMBER

We have all talked about struggles, but your pain can be replaced with comfort and love. One may hesitate to return love when there is no invested interest or reciprocation. An invested love calls for a commitment to the end and that is where the Bridal Chamber awaits your presence.

When others do not see the pain, the experiences can be hidden underneath the shadows. This is where pain can then become well preserved and wrapped in your innermost being; which is not at all good.

The heavenly Bridegroom is calling you by name to embrace this burden. He is saying in the quietness of love,

"Come unto me, all you that are weary and are carrying heavy burdens, and I will give you rest," (Matthew 11:28).

Jesus is saying, you are my sweet love,

"Take my yoke upon you and learn of me; for I am meek and lowly in heart: and ye shall find rest unto your souls," (Matthew 11:29, KJV).

He is saying many times, I will not cause you pain like those imposters who profess to love you. For "*I am the way, the truth and the life*." (John 14:6)

Imposters engage in self-interest without guilt. But as the True Lover of your being; follow Him into the Bridal Chamber where you will receive His unconditional love, healing, and comfort.

REFLECTIONS

What experiences from your pain may cause you to hide underneath the shadows?

_____

_____

_____

_____

_____

How have relational experiences with imposters made you feel about receiving unconditional love?

_____

_____

_____

_____

What investments will you make towards your healing with the True Lover of your soul?

_____

_____

_____

_____

**Do not hide in the shadow
of your pain, let it come forth**

NO LEFT TURN

Love Empowers You to Stay Above Your Pain, Not Below It

REAL LOVE IN THE CHAMBER

Now we come to real love. Real love is found in the heavenly Bridal Chamber, and it nurtures and nourishes authentic truth. This truth is centered in meditative peace which encompasses stillness, quietness, reflection, and the gratification of God's heartbeat.

Meditative peace embraces the essence of being present within and being connected to the core of your heart. The Bridegroom awaits your presence.

"But those who wait for the Lord shall renew their strength, they shall mount up with wings like eagles, they shall run and not be weary, they shall walk and not faint" (Isaiah 40:31).

On your purposeful path to the Bridal Chamber, the authentic engagement of love becomes decisive and clear. Jeremiah 31:3 says,

"I have loved you with an everlasting love; therefore I have continued my faithfulness to you,"

Take note, this love here is the signature or hallmark of God's devotion to you!

REFLECTIONS

What meditative peace do you need to embrace?

_____

_____

_____

_____

_____

_____

What would you like to experience in your authentic engagement of love in the Bridal Chamber?

_____

_____

_____

_____

_____

_____

Write out a prayer to God about those areas on your purposeful path.

_____

_____

_____

_____

_____

_____

RAHAB'S PAIN TO JOY

A prime example of pain being replaced by joy can be found in the story of Rahab. Rahab in the Book of Joshua was an outcast, a harlot or a sinful woman who was also in the genealogy of Jesus. In the perseverance of her journey, she aspired from victim to victor, from rejection to acceptance, and from fearful to courageous.

Rahab may have been written off as a loose woman or lady of the evening; who was purged and forgiven by God and shared in the royal line of Jesus. Despite her past, she became united with the people of Israel who served the True and Living God. She was determined to follow after Him and change her ways. She was thought to be unworthy of entering the Chamber. However, she succeeded in becoming the mother of Boaz, who later married Ruth (Matthew 1:5).

There are those who would have loved to see Rahab cast into the abyss, instead of the Bridegroom's Chamber. Rahab was criticized for not fitting in with the higher-class and societal superiors who disliked others in the lower-class. Her inner turmoil of rejection and trauma by others was painful. However, she persisted in her devotion and obedience. Today, she is counted faithful; along with many others in the Bible such as Abraham and Moses.

"By faith the harlot Rahab perished not with those who believed not, when she had received the spies with peace," (Hebrews 11:31, KJV).

To accept oneself is to believe in oneself. Remember, there is no discrimination in the Chamber of God's heart—only unconditional love. So come one; come all, come broken, come wounded, come stained or indifferent. He will carry us in the womb of his very being with a heart of compassionate love. Therefore, come as you are...

All are welcomed in the Bridal Chamber

"There is therefore no condemnation for those who are in Christ Jesus; who do not walk according to the flesh, but according to the Spirit," (Romans 8:1, NKJV).

REFLECTIONS

Have you ever felt like an outcast or been rejected; how did that make you feel?

_____

_____

_____

_____

_____

What ways do you combat negative criticism?

_____

_____

_____

_____

_____

Describe what "come as you are" looks like in your life; as you move towards experiencing God's unconditional love in the Bridal Chamber.

_____

_____

_____

_____

_____

Allow your pain to cross the path to healing

GREEN LIGHT

Be Present in the Midst of Your Pain

BEING CENTERED IN THE CHAMBER

Are you aware that your thoughts, pride, obstacles, distractions, fear, or even pain can prevent you from being present? This sometimes can serve as your first line of defense in attendance. As a result, you're always in a continuous state of motion or doing; avoiding the here and now. But just as Rahab trusted in God and was faithful until the end of her life, it is important to center your heart in the Bridal Chamber. This allows your heart to be one with the Bridegroom, unified and joined together. The soul, body, mind, and spirit; all can gravitate to an eternal love like no other. In this Chamber, the external world does not matter, but internal love captivates authentic truth.

The Bridegroom is calling you to the Chamber of life and awaits your union. Only He can provide you with eternal love that is perpetual. It is in this union that you become one with Him.

The songwriter, Charlotte Elliott, penned a familiar and glorious hymn of invitation that you can adopt into your life:

"Just as I am and waiting not. To rid my soul of one dark blot. To thee whose blood can cleanse each spot. O lamb of God I come, I come."

Remember this, the invitation of eternal love has been extended and awaits you in the Chamber. Will you come today?

REFLECTIONS

Can you sense the Lord's desire for you to come in union with Him?

_____

_____

_____

_____

_____

_____

What are your limitations from doing so?

_____

_____

_____

_____

_____

_____

Take a moment to develop this union by reading and reciting this scripture aloud, "If you confess with your lips that Jesus is Lord and believe in your heart that God raised him from the dead, you will be saved. For one believes with the heart and so is justified, and one confesses with the mouth and so is saved," (Rom 10:9-10).

THE VEIL OF FORGIVENESS

Every believer has the ability to experience the joy of forgiveness from sin. The veil of forgiveness came at a great price. After Jesus' death, the temple veil was torn in two.

"Then Jesus cried again with a loud voice and breathed his last. At that moment, the curtain of the temple was torn in two, from top to bottom. The earth shook and the rocks were split," (Matthew 27:50-51).

This represents the forgiveness of our sins and Christ as the only path to God the Father. His crucifixion allowed you freedom and access to life, love, and forgiveness. Jesus does not live in an ivory tower made by the hands of man, but He lives in the heart of His creation which is you.

"But we have this treasure in earthen vessels, to show that the transcendent power belongs to God and not to us" (2 Corinthians 4:7).

Christ awaits your entrance into the Holy Chamber just as you are. He welcomes you inside His dwelling place beyond the veil, which is no longer earthly, but a resting place in God's presence.

"You show me the path of life. In your presence there is fullness of joy; in your right hand are pleasures forevermore," (Psalm 16:11).

The old ways and barriers are obsolete, and a new path is made with confidence to the Holy Chamber:

"For we do not have a high priest who cannot sympathize with our weaknesses, but One who has been tempted in all things just as we are, yet without sin." (Hebrews 4:15 NASB).

Christ Himself is our representation. The temple was a picture of things on the horizon which pointed to Jesus. His death now allowed forgiveness and free access to the Chamber of His heart. The way of forgiveness is opened to all humanity, and you are invited to embrace the fullness of His love today. For it has been declared,

"We have confidence to enter the Most Holy Place by the blood of Jesus Christ by a new and living way through the curtain, which is his body," (Hebrews 10:19-29).

He has already set the stage with the veil of forgiveness, you are no longer slaves to sin; instead, you are free to love and be loved.

REFLECTIONS

What can hinder you from experiencing the joy of forgiveness from sin?

_____

_____

_____

_____

_____

_____

Make a list of who or what to forgive to walk in this level of freedom.

_____

_____

_____

_____

_____

_____

Describe what it looks like to you to love and be loved.

_____

_____

_____

_____

_____

_____

RESILIENCE IN THE PAIN OF FORGIVENESS

Being still in the presence of forgiveness is triumphing through pain. It takes courage to forgive. Unforgiveness will cause you to miss opportunities, live in a perpetual prison of rehearsed pain or inhibit you from moving forward to embrace the fullness of your purpose. Therefore, you have to forgive those in your past, your present and sometimes yourself; in order to step into your future. However, you can overcome your pain by the truth you know; because the Truth will set you free.

Beloved, it is the Truth found in the Word of God that gives you resilience and brings liberation. Do not allow your pain to stop you from receiving all that the Father has for you.

"Wisdom is the principal thing; therefore... in all your getting, get [His] understanding," (Proverbs 4:7 KJV).

You have a choice: you can be crippled or walk in the freedom of truth; for where the Spirit of the Lord is, there is liberty, (2 Corinthians 3:17 KJV).

As a result, by simply letting it go and leaning into God is where you will find resilience. Release your pain of forgiveness today:

"Stand up, take up your mat and walk!"

(John 5:8)

REFLECTIONS

What will discourage you about your situation that keeps you from embracing God's truth; that brings about resilience?

_____

_____

_____

_____

_____

List who or what you need to forgive to walk in freedom ?

_____

_____

_____

_____

_____

Make a choice today. Write out a statement expressing whether or not you will stay crippled in unforgiveness or have the courage to release any resentment or bitterness in your heart.

_____

_____

_____

_____

_____

Do not walk in the shadow of your pain, let it go

Welcome to Your New Journey

Rescue Your Pain

Broken But Silent

T he Chamber is a safe place that awaits the brokenness of our hearts; as silence reveals the strength of it. Silence is often seen as a sign of weakness. But in the Bridal Chamber, silence is a strength that emanates truth. It is through brokenness that silence develops who we are becoming; which is beyond the capacity of who we are in ourselves.

Scripture tells us in 2 Corinthians 12:10b, *"when I am weak, then I am strong."* Once we have accepted Christ as our personal Savior, we have the power of His Resurrection within us. Therefore, we will no longer need to be silent because we will be changed. More interesting, we can follow the example of Christ when He walked the earth. He was silent when He experienced many things. Yet, He kept his eyes focused on the Heavenly Father. Now the same brokenness that Jesus felt when he died on the cross for our sins, can unlock a treasure for us if we will trust Him.

He is the One who was accused, spat upon, beaten, and mocked but He remained silent in truth. He stood steady in the middle of chaos, as the sacrificial lamb.

"He was oppressed and treated harshly, yet he never said a word. He was led like a lamb to the

slaughter. And as a sheep is silent before the shearers, he did not open his mouth," (Isaiah 53:7, NLT). Also, Jesus was led to trial before the high priest, but Matthew 26:63 says, *"Jesus was silent."*

Take heed, America is broken. Our homes are broken, the political system is broken, the educational system is broken, the health system is broken, our children are broken and violence is rampant with chaos and destruction in humanity. But despite all the devastation that we are experiencing, we can learn to move forward with hope and healing. For pain is something that we often avoid but serves as a necessary step; that surrenders to freedom.

Jesus holds the keys to bring us to this place of liberty. Although life will find a way of stretching us for a purpose; many are crushed on the inside, hiding behind their smiles and questioning themselves. But He unlocks the treasures of who we truly are. The investment of who we will be, was already paid for on the Cross; which allows us to continuously strengthen our faithfulness to God. In this Holy place, it is He who heals, it is He who loves, and it is He who can empower us. Therefore, we no longer have to stay broken, tattered, stuck; nor silent because when we *are* weak, then He *is* strong [in us]!

REFLECTIONS

Describe the pain in your broken place that has kept you silent.

_____

_____

_____

_____

_____

_____

Share ways that you have tried to work through this process.

_____

_____

_____

_____

_____

_____

What ways can your brokenness serve as a catalyst for change?

_____

_____

_____

_____

_____

_____

THE SHED BLOOD FOR PAIN

W hat can we learn from the shed blood of Christ? Christ died for all, and His blood cleanses us from all unrighteousness. As you walk towards the Chamber, it brings comfort to a wounded soul.

"But if we walk in the light as He Himself is in the light, we have fellowship with one another, and the blood of Jesus his Son cleanses us from all sin," (1 John 1:7).

Washing by the blood promotes cleansing from our impurities through the acceptance of His unconditional love. It renews the process of our humanity in restoring new life. Even though you may walk through the valley of the shadow of death, which feels like the shedding of blood, amplified by intense pain, or engulfed by the surrounding darkness; step into the light of hope.

The Son of God endured tremendous pain; whose blood was shed with the sting of a whip, the piercing of nails, the spear in his side, and the thorns on his head. He endured this painful sacrifice on the cross, just for you.

For it is written, "...He was wounded for our transgressions, crushed for our iniquities; upon him was the punishment that made us whole, and by his bruises we are healed," (Isaiah 53:5).

Take note, it is the release of His pain that led to the healing of our pain. For the blood of the Lamb cleanses the soul and heals the wounds. Accept your healing and allow the essence of His love to guide and soothe you. Whereas, it was always His purpose to renew our humanity and restore new life.

Reflections

Write out a prayer that addresses areas in your life that need cleansing.

_____

_____

_____

_____

_____

Recite your prayer out loud to reinforce and strengthen your faith.

_____

_____

_____

_____

_____

Take a moment to describe your renewal and healing from God's love.

_____

_____

_____

_____

_____

The restoration of pain creates hope

On Your Mark, Get Set, Go!

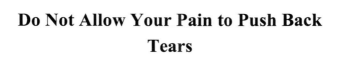

Do Not Allow Your Pain to Push Back Tears

When Tears Become Blood

When *Tears Become Blood,* no one can handle this by themselves; although they try. You will **always** need the Lord because it comes to destroy, or imprison you. It's an unwelcomed turmoil or agony that flows deep. Sometimes, you never know who you can trust; or, if you want to live or die. But never let it break you. You can turn your anger around because there's a lesson from this sorrow. Yes, God knows He can trust you with this level of pain as His witness.

When Jesus was in the Garden of Gethsemane, praying before he went to be crucified, the Bible says that, *"he prayed very fervently; and His sweat became like drops of blood,"* (Luke 22:44, KJV). Lorraine Wright, a close friend and therapist; specializing in grief and trauma, stated that she has "worked with people who have experienced pain that sometimes *seem* like drops of blood. Even so, there is a parallel that has been discovered by connecting their current symptoms to that of their past trauma. This technique is called Eye Movement Desensitization and Reprocessing (EMDR); developed by Francine Shapiro. This assists individuals in having more "clarity" of the trauma and changing the way they see themselves."

Can you imagine Jesus' crucifixion that represented the greatest expression of His blood, tears and God's love? He sacrificed His very young life for *all* humanity. Here, He cried out in agony with perpetual tears. However, before He died on the Cross, He felt like the Father had forsaken him as He took on the sins of the world.

Understand, pain can weigh you down and slow your journey to the Bridal Chamber. Do not allow it to hinder you. This is where you are accompanied across the threshold; across the entrance point to where your heart will be lifted. Here, you are surrounded by His healing light and unconditional love. This love is what guides you through the pain; where you are made whole *and* given strength.

For example, when we experience the death of a loved one, our pain becomes our disconnect to the world and sometimes to God. In 2021, I experienced that disconnect with the pain and grief of losing my spouse of over 40 years and sometimes; we may not always know how to find the balance. David Kessler, a renowned author, once stated, "We grieve because we love." But in our grieving process, the only thing that can be easily felt is the overshadowing of pain. However, all are welcomed to come to the Bridal Chamber. Here, I'm learning that love does not *stop* because of death; love *continues* as a result of it.

So, in this safe place, self-reflection and silence allows for the surrender of pain, suffering, and the darkness of our souls. A place where we know that our struggle *is* real, our experiences *were* real, and our memories *are* real. This is where we find ourselves wrestling, devastated or anguished with open wounds from a life shattering moment.

Now, He is calling you to this place, even in your lowest thoughts or doubts in Him because He can identify. Jesus was, "a man of sorrows, and acquainted with grief," (Isaiah 53:3). He understands your suffering, distress, agony, fear, questions or despair. However, it's His beautiful act of outright love and forgiveness, that you now have access to this holy place. This is where He finds you: lost, speechless, broken, confused or alone. But He doesn't want you to bleed anymore. It is His good pleasure to bless you and heal your heart… for He loves you!

Therefore, take back your power and grab hold of what God is offering you today. This is your set time.Why hesitate? Bring Him your tears of blood and rise up as a resilient warrior who triumphs through trauma.

For Jesus said, *"Let not your heart be troubled: ye believe in God, believe also in me,"* (John 14:1, KJV).

So my dear friend, it's okay to surrender; for *"by His stripes we are [already] healed,"* (Isaiah 53:5, NKJV). So believe, His hand is at work in your life and *you will see the goodness of the Lord in the land of the living.* (Psalm 27:13)

REFLECTIONS

In the dark pain of your tears, what are your stumbling blocks that prevent you from receiving healing?

_____

_____

_____

_____

_____

_____

What will it take for you to bring everything to this safe place?

_____

_____

_____

_____

_____

_____

Write out the areas or ways you can surrender your all today.

_____

_____

_____

_____

_____

_____

A Purposeful Path Towards
the Chamber

There is no pathway that does not direct you to a place on your journey in life. Some paths may lead you to the edge of spiritual transcendence or greatness and others to destruction. *"And make straight paths for your feet..."* (Hebrews 12:2-13). Every step you take, is either moving you forward or backwards, but nonetheless, you are still moving.

Why not move towards your purposeful path to the Chamber that awaits your destiny?

Jesus has already declared your purposeful path. The Apostle Paul says, *"Be imitators of me, as I am of Christ,"* (1 Corinthians 11:1). Christ will carry you in the Chamber of His heart as you go forth on your journey. If you have pain, do not deny it, but grow from it. Remember Jesus says, *"Come to me, all you that are weary and are carrying heavy burdens, and I will give you rest. Take my yoke upon you and learn from me; for I am gentle and humble in heart, and you will find rest for your souls,"* (Matthew 11:28-29).

There is rest in the Chamber as you strive for respite, recovery, strength, clarity, joy or vision. His love awaits you in this place and provides clarity of your purpose. For Hebrews 4:9-11 tells us that, *"There remaineth therefore a rest to the people of God..."*

For that reason, take ownership of your purposeful path. But you first must believe that you have a path with purpose. Proverbs 3:6 states, *"In all your ways acknowledge him, and he will make straight your paths."* Thus, boldly declare in Him:

I *Am* Loved... I *Am* Healed... I *Am* Free... I *Have* Hope... I *Have* Dreams... and I *Have* Purpose!

Your ownership is a declaration of all that is being discovered and materialized. You can now courageously say with confidence:

I Believe ~ I Belong ~ I Trust ~ I Embrace ~ and I Am Empowered

So remember, your presence with Him will reveal this to you. Pursue it! Whereas, you were created to fulfill your God - given purpose; according to His plan.

84

REFLECTIONS

Identify today any areas of your life where you need rest?

_____

_____

_____

_____

_____

What steps are you currently taking in your situation that will move you forward or backwards?

_____

_____

_____

_____

_____

How can you be intentional in pursuing God's presence in receiving His plan for your life?

_____

_____

_____

_____

_____

Do Not Allow Pain to Own You

DROP YOUR BAGS

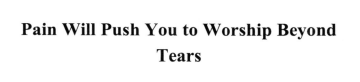

Pain Will Push You to Worship Beyond Tears

WORSHIP IN THE CHAMBER

One thing that is paramount and needed in the Bridal Chamber is worship. Worship is available and ready to embrace you in the secret place of the Father's heart. This is where you will experience His love, His burden, His joy, His freedom, and His glory.

The truth of worship is that it delivers you to who you are becoming throughout the process of healing. The Bridegroom is saying, bring everything into the Chamber;

"Take my yoke upon you, and learn from me; for I am gentle and humble in heart, and you will find rest for your souls," (Matthew 11:29).

For the Lord wants to carry your heart, your pain, your desire, disappointments, and unforgiveness. Therefore my dear beloved, hold on to the promise of;

"Come to me, all you that are weary and burdened, and I will give you rest," (Matthew 11:28, NASB).

In releasing your true worship to Him, you are allowing the embodiment of the Father's heart, His being, and His aroma to fill you afresh; with the essence of a new fragrance. Moreover,

"We love because he first loved us," (1 John 4:19).

Therefore, come into the Chamber as the Father awaits your very presence with joy and give you what you are needing. Considering, He is ready to engage you; for He "... *is spirit, and those who worship Him must worship in spirit and truth,"* (John 4:24).

REFLECTIONS

Describe any challenges that would hinder you from encountering a time of worship with the Lord?

_____

_____

_____

_____

_____

_____

What benefits are you looking to experience when you enter this place?

_____

_____

_____

_____

_____

_____

List how you can bring worship into your daily routine.

_____

_____

_____

_____

_____

_____

COME DANCE WITH ME

One essential element of worship is worship in dance. If you have ever felt deliverance or victory, you have danced or wanted to dance in some way. In the Old Testament, we are reminded of King David who saw the Ark of the Covenant and danced freely before the Lord with all his might. (see 1 Samuel 6)

One way to release pain is to dance. We can go through tremendous difficulties with ourselves and with others as a way to try to cover up. We may even try to cover it from our significant other because our instinct is to support and protect them by being a guardian.

Sometimes in life, protecting the pain is like wearing military gear in order to protect oneself from an unexpected ambush. This is an experience I had while serving in the United States Army. When the warfare was over, the gears came off. But we were never designed to carry such horrific pain alone; even if we all have our own cross to bear. Nonetheless, we need to free ourselves and *let go* of the pain!

Today the Father wants to fully embrace you to draw out your pain through His love. He has an eternal love that never dries up and it *is* forever. He desires to exchange your gear and mend your wounded heart that has been dripping with sweat and blood. In this Secret Chamber, there is an oil of healing that never runs dry. It is a continuous flow to the broken places. A fresh oil that flows once you surrender your tears of blood - woundedness in exchange for wholeness.

In this place, you are releasing a cleansing of dead and toxic poison from your system. Through this system, the Trinity -The Father, The Son, and The Holy Spirit, desires to dance with you to bring restoration to every essence of your being. The Father is saying, Come dance with me. I want to take you places where you have never been before. This is a new journey from the Throne Room of my heart to yours. Let me dance with you my child, I desire to replace your pain with joy, your heaviness with praise; to give you beauty for ashes. (Isaiah 61:3 KJV)

Therefore Beloved, your appropriate response should be:

"You have turned my mourning into dancing; you have taken off my sackcloth and clothed me with joy, so that my soul may praise you and not be silent. LORD my God, I will give thanks to you forever,"
(Psalm 30:11-12).

Now this is an eternal dance that will be one of *fire and love.* For only He can give you flowers in place of

your sorrow, oil in place of tears, and a joyous praise
in place of a broken heart. (Isaiah 61:3 CEV)

REFLECTIONS

Are you willing to dance as a sign of victory over your circumstance?

_____

_____

_____

_____

_____

What do you need to release to make this exchange for this level of freedom?

_____

_____

_____

_____

_____

List some of the benefits that you are looking forward to experiencing with the Lord?

_____

_____

_____

_____

_____

Release the toxic pain and dance to your freedom

LIBERTY AWAITS

Dare to Go Beyond the Veil of Pain to Freedom

BEYOND THE VEIL

Beloved, you have arrived! This is the final stage of fully stepping into the Bridal Chamber. Make sure you turn away or abandon all ungodly behaviors and intentions; in both your motives and practices. Then, turn to God and walk in obedience.

Now, take a moment, look around and inhale the aroma of His presence. Do not fear; be intimidated or hesitate from stepping into your rightful position as a bride. It does not matter *who* you are, *where* you have been, or *what* you have done. God loves *All* humanity and wants to fully restore you in **Him**!

For that reason, *we are accepted in the Beloved! He is so rich in grace and mercy that He purchased our freedom with the blood of his Son and forgave our sins* (Ephesians 1:6,7, NLT).

Remember, life can trip you up. However today, we come to serve notice on the evil one; that everything he used to cause pain or tried to break you is EVICTED in the name of Jesus! Therefore, disappointment *has to go,* abuse *has to go*, illness *has to go*, rejection *has to go,* mental anguish *has to go*, division *has to go,* suicide *has to go*, and pride ***has to go***! Right now, *your help comes from the LORD; the Maker of Heaven and earth.*

For He who watches over you, will never sleep nor slumber (see Psalm 121).

You *are* restored, **you** *are* set free, and **you** *are* being elevated in Christ to walk in limitless grace, love, and freedom. Do not allow yesterday to keep you from God's goodness because He is doing a new thing. He promises to give you beauty for ashes for your painful experience.

Now your invitation has been waiting for your acceptance and arrival. The Father says, *"Yea, I have loved you with an everlasting love: therefore, with loving kindness have I drawn thee" (Jeremiah 31:3, KJV).* I am pursuing you beyond the veil and you are not alone. **I AM** your Shepherd, you shall not want, (Psalms 23:1, KJV). I have always been with you; orchestrating your life strategically, intentionally, and purposefully to bring you to myself because **I AM** Sovereign. **I AM** Alpha and Omega - I know your end from the beginning. So now you can rest, because **I AM** the **Lover** of your soul, the **Lifter** of your head, and the **Light** unto your pathway who will love you *forever and always*!

Congratulations!

It took bravery, determination, and endurance to get to this place. You *are* courageous! You *are* triumphant and You *are* Victorious!

Celebrate your win and walk it out.

"Be confident in this, He who began a good work in you will perform it until the day of Jesus Christ. "(Philippians 1:6)

Therefore, let this be your confirmation; that the Father is *always* mindful of who you are. So remember, you are resilient and when you are in Christ, you are a new creature. Therefore, embrace your transformation, put on your super hero cape, hold your head up high and walk in your victory. You have crossed over to the other side.

Now go, pursue and achieve your dreams.

But first, take a moment to document your goals in the coming future, share ways that you will implement these outcomes and *always* give the Father glory.

You Got This...

EPILOGUE

Dear Friends,

We are living in a place where pain and trauma has almost taken havoc in this world today. But we have an opportunity to come face-to-face and acknowledge ownership of our power in Christ.

Freedom only comes when we allow the heart to challenge the head and when the head connects with God's heart. For Truth liberates humanity like no other and invites you to dance with an eternal fire of love. The love of Christ was given in exchange for our healing. It liberates through pain, emotional trauma, imprisonment of the mind, and hope for tomorrow.

"Love never fails…," (1 Corinthians 13:8, KJV)

Recognize that the love of the Father has called you beyond your pain to embrace the process of healing from the bondage to freedom. You are Not alone; you have taken the step into the Chamber of the Bridegroom. Your freedom was always awaiting to empower you on this purposeful journey. The Father pursued you beyond the veil for your response. Now He states, *"Come unto me, all ye that labour and are heavy laden, and I will give you rest…you shall find*

100

rest unto your souls. For my yoke is easy, and my burden is light," (Matthew 11:30).

Therefore, celebrate your freedom from pain to praise and embrace the prayer of salvation to your new beginning.

For we declare boldly, *"...if any man be in Christ, he is a new creature: old things have passed away; behold, all things have become new,"* (2 Corinthians 5:17, KJV).

A Gift To You

Salvation is a free gift from God our Heavenly Father. If you are ready to receive this free gift, pray this prayer: Lord Jesus, I confess my sins and ask for your forgiveness.

"For he says, at an acceptable time I have listened to you, and on a day of salvation I have helped you. See, now is the acceptable time; see, now is the day of salvation!" (2 Corinthians 6:2). Therefore, I acknowledge You as Lord in my life; I believe with my heart that God raised You from the dead and today, I am saved. (Romans 10:9) Amen.

The contact you made with God has already been heard before your words were ever expressed. He delights in having a real conversation with you. You have expressed many things through the release of your words. Even as David expressed in prayer to God. He indicated,

"Have mercy upon me, O God, according to Your lovingkindness; according to the multitude of Your tender mercies, blot out my transgressions. Wash me thoroughly from my iniquity, and cleanse me from my sin. Behold, You desire truth in the inward parts, and in the hidden part You will make me to know wisdom. Purge me with hyssop, and I shall be clean; Wash me, and I shall be whiter than snow. Make me hear joy and gladness, that the bones You have broken may rejoice. Create in me a clean heart, O God, and renew a steadfast spirit within me. Do not cast me away from Your presence, and do not take Your Holy Spirit from me. Restore to me the joy of Your salvation, and uphold me by Your generous Spirit" (Psalm 51:1,2, 6-8,10-12 NKJV).

Lord, receive my heartfelt prayer and forgiveness. For without you, I will still be alone and left in my pain. Amen

Reminders for Your Journey

Guidance

Guidance is defined by Oxford Languages as a vice or information aimed at resolving a problem or difficulty; especially as given by someone in authority. Normally, during any emergency one seeks the help of a friend or calls 911.

However, there is someone who will help guide and carry your pain from past experiences; and that someone is the Lord Jesus Christ. It is written in Psalm 32:8, *"I will instruct you and teach you the way you should go; I will counsel you with my eye upon you."*

Freedom

Freedom is the state of being free or at liberty rather than in confinement or under physical restraints. It is the power or right to act, speak or think as one wants; without hindrance or external control.

In your pain or brokenness, truth can be revealed to free yourself or others; for it produces a liberation from uncertainty, doubt, and falsehood. Therefore, you don't have to be held in captivity with disbelief, but you can be liberated in your pain. For it is written, "*you have been called to live in freedom, my brothers and sisters. But don't use your freedom to satisfy your sinful nature, instead, use your freedom to serve one another in love*" (Galatians 5:13 NLT).

Love

"*We know that all things work together for good for those who love God, who are called according to his purpose,*" (Romans 8:28). You are called to a purposeful love that comes from the Father that is unconditional and true.

Imposters will call you to a counterfeit love that isn't necessarily genuine or meet the true essence of the Father's love. They operate in self-interest without guilt, promises with no fulfillment and often short-lived. But there is a Faithful Lover; one who made a sacrifice for you, guaranteeing everlasting life, and offering an unfailing love without an eviction notice.

Remember in your pain, he desires to bathe and shower you with a commitment to you always; which simply means… "Love never ends. But as for prophecies, they will come to an end; as for tongues, they will cease; as for knowledge, it will come to an end," (1 Corinthians 13:8). Therefore, embrace the heart of the Father for

...God is love (1 John 4:8)

Support

Support means to bear all or part of the weight; to uphold or defend as valid or right; to give assistance or pay the costs. Consequently, a supportive love can keep you standing during the time when you're ready to faint. But there is one who will support you if there is a void; and help you endure bravely or quietly. What an awesome reassurance to know that you will be supported and surrounded in love by the one who has paid the price. Jesus makes the declaration by stating, "*I will never leave you or forsake you. Therefore, you can say with confidence, "The Lord is my helper; I will not be afraid. What can anyone do to me?"* (Hebrews 13:5b,6)

Alignment

For "the spirit of the Lord GOD is upon me, because the LORD has anointed me; he has sent me to bring good news to the oppressed, to bind up the brokenhearted, to proclaim liberty to the captives, and release to the prisoners," (Isaiah 61:1).

You have an open invitation to be free from sin; the burden of guilt, depression, or shame. Therefore, come into agreement and walk in your freedom. Learn to take ownership of your rightful place as stated, *"So if the Son makes you free, you will be free indeed" (John 8:36,* KJV). When the Son has set you free, you are no longer a slave to what happened. Jesus sets the stage for forgiveness and gives liberty to all who will receive. The invitation of this alignment with Him awaits you in the Bridal Chamber. Take courage and embrace the benefits of being one in the spirit with the Lord. You have the *Green Light; now be free!*

Restoration

After your affliction, one can only hope for the possibilities of repair or reestablishment. God's restoration is always in abundance and there is hope in being restored. There were times where you were encapsulated; confined in a tight space with no life-giving breath to your pain. But you have earned your return to restoration through the blood shed of Jesus Christ; restoring you back to God's original design.

He offers a blood covenant of forgiveness, healing, hope, and restoration. For Jesus declared, "This is my blood of the covenant, which is poured out for many," (Mark 14:24). Therefore, accept your gift of restoration today and take ownership of your house. *He already paid the price and He paid it all!*

Renewal

Today God wants to offer you a new beginning. You can be renewed which is defined as, "The replacing or repair of something that is worn out, run-down, or broken."

Pain can slow you down on your purposeful path towards your true destination. You have been tired; carrying a heavy heart, disconnected or shed tears of blood with the essence of your strength. But it is time to gear up and take charge of your journey.

As a runner there is a starting point - *On your mark, get set, Go!* Push forward to take ownership of the prize that awaits you. It is a place of renewal for what has been broken. Now with that being the case, don't hesitate but take a leap of faith and finish well.

"Be renewed in the spirit of your minds" (Ephesians 4:23).

Dance

2 Corinthians 3:17 states that, *"Now the Lord is the Spirit, and where the Spirit of the Lord is, there is freedom."* Dance is a rhythmic sequence of steps with liberty of movement.

Therefore, it is time to drop your bags and embrace a new dance of freedom with the trinity - the Father, Son, and Holy Spirit. He desires for you to release everything and be refreshed and renewed; turning your pain into gain, your hopelessness into joy, and warfare into worship.

So, I dare you to change partners today with heaviness for a new dance of joy declaring, *"You have turned my mourning into dancing; you loose my sackcloth and clothe me with gladness,"* (Psalm 30:11, ESV). For it's now time to dance in freedom with the Lord who desires to waltz with you.

From the Publisher's Desk...

TRIUMPH OVER YOUR
TRIGGERS

"Though you have made me see troubles, many and bitter, you will restore my life again; from the depths of the earth you will again bring me up." Psalm 71:20
NIV

As you read *"When Tears Become Blood,"* prayerfully it will speak to the heart of the survivor. The process is not a "one size fits all" but it can make you feel vulnerable. Yet it offers you a journey in a relationship to experience a love or a refuge that you may have never encountered with the One who can not only replenish your soul; but also save your life! This is not about erasing what happened but walking you to a place where you can grab hold of your faith; embrace the love and freedom of the Lord and live your blessed life.

However, as you *Triumph Through Pain*, it is filled with many ups and downs which can seem like an unpredictable path. Your triggers may come as a result of a death, divorce, mistreatment, betrayal, rejection, abuse, loss of independence, words, or an accident. But there are no warnings given when something will trigger a reaction in you. For that reason, it is so crucial that you identify your triggers and learn how to manage them.

A trigger by one definition simply suggests a call-to-action; or a response to trauma that can bring on or worsen symptoms. They are identified as cues, signals, or nudges that motivate you to do something or exhibit a particular behavior.

But the good news is that your triggers don't have to run your life. Therefore, it is important to learn from them so you can eventually overcome, heal or move forward. Nonetheless, avoiding them is not an option! You can experience the Lord's grace and peace; not to mention many health benefits as you gain control over these prompts. But your healing is achievable.

However, there are a few types of triggers to take note of and one in particular is internal triggers which can be considered personal. These are factors that come from within an individual and based on thoughts, feelings, and emotions that bring about specific behaviors. They can include guilt, shame, anger, happiness, depression, nervousness, boredom, sleepiness, etc. Sometimes, your trigger will come in the form of an internal question. This is where you find yourself always looking back or wondering if you could have done something different. The only problem here is that you will find yourself going in circles and never really have an answer.

But perhaps the most popular of all triggers are external. These are environmental components that are easily manipulated and can cause things to be prompted. They mainly come from outside factors that will nudge you to do something. Some are hot triggers like a text message that acts as an indicator to take action now. Others can be considered a cold trigger used as a subtle persuasion to act like a commercial that entices you to purchase their product the next time you're hungry. But there are many things like drugs, music, social events, uncomfortable environments, financial struggles, stressful or toxic people that can all serve as external triggers. They have the potential to be difficult for you or take you back places that you rather not revisit. In any event, these triggers can be a spark which motivates you to act; serve as a signal acting like a reminder of what you can do or a facilitator that helps you complete an action under the guidance of a professional; like a therapist.

At the same time, can you imagine being triggered as a spiritually sensitive person who is in pain? It's almost like you grieve twice! In social settings, you may have a hard time because you can pick up what's going on in the atmosphere or in the hearts of others, good or bad. You may often sense, smell, see, or hear things that may be none of your business after walking into a room. It's almost like you pick up on the hidden war inside of others; while trying to reconcile what you see. This can be overwhelming sometimes so you may isolate yourself a lot because of your sensitivity in the spirit realm. You interact from the heart; listening to how you respond to people or an environment and what they carry. This is when you utilize discernment; a gift from God where you may understand or know something through the guidance of the Holy Spirit. It comes from prayer, reading and meditating on the Word of God and growing in wisdom.

A few examples in the bible include 2 Kings 4:9 that shows you how the Shunammite woman discerned Elisha was a prophet of God. Also, in John 4:19-42, you can read the story of the Samaritan woman at the well's encounter with Jesus Christ. She had perceived that he was more than the average man.

So having discernment demonstrates insight and wisdom beyond what we see or hear. It helps us make distinctions to recognize truth. For that reason, it is imperative to have intimacy with the Lord who is Omniscient and All Knowing. He is the One who becomes your confidant or best friend; who you share your feelings with and go to at the end of the day. Otherwise you run the risk of being triggered and not being able to cope. But Jesus is the Answer and a Keeper who is able to keep you from falling, and present you faultless before the presence of His glory (Jude 1:24)

Therefore, spending intentional time with the Lord can help you to let go of all that you have experienced, renew your strength, recharge and receive the love of God.

That is why it is so important that you continue and mature in your relationship with Him because it also helps you exercise self-control even when you find yourself susceptible to being irritated. Remember, the enemy will do his best and even work overtime to trip you up; for his objective to steal, kill and destroy has never changed.

Thankfully, it is the Holy Spirit who helps you navigate your triggers and gives you power to live successfully! You are not alone. No matter how bad you're struggling, you can still have victory; resilience in triumphing over your triggers and enjoy life in Christ. For Jesus said, "in the world ye shall have trouble: but be of good cheer; I have overcome the world. (John 16:33)

One way you can successfully navigate your triggers is to make a list or create a plan of action, thereby, recognizing your triggers. Identify any toxic thoughts and behaviors associated with your pain and take note. Isaiah 26:3 reminds us that He will keep us in perfect peace, whose mind is stayed on Him. Ask yourself, what areas do you find yourself focusing on the most? Once identified, this can help you close the door or manage your triggers better.

Then replace your triggers. One of the ways you can do this is to substitute your negative thoughts because what you believe, you have the potential to become! For Proverbs 23:7 says, as a man thinketh in his heart, so is he. Whenever you are having an experience, look for a bible verse related to freedom in the area you are struggling in. You can replace your triggers when you know what God says about it.

Also, learn to recite the Word of God over your triggers. When you start to make the exchange and openly declare the Word; announcing it over your trigger, you're taking steps to overcome. This is not a new concept, the Word of God is like a sword that can be used to declare your freedom, dispel the lies, or defeat the enemy. That's why Jesus would say, , "it is written, man shall not live by bread alone but every word that proceeds out of the mouth of God (Matt 4:4). So I ask you today, what are you speaking over your life?

God's Word is living & powerful (Heb 4:12), and He watches over His Word to perform it (Jer. 1:12). Therefore, never allow anyone or anything power over you; when you have worked so hard to be or do better!

The Lord wants you to experience victory and freedom in every area of your life. Do what you have to do to manage or overcome. You can prepare yourself by doing a reality check or a self-reflection. Learn to own your triggers by being responsible for your actions. Do the work by having a plan of action or get help by speaking to a professional.

But be strong in the Lord and in the power of his might. (Ephesians 6:10). Be mindful, put on the full armor of God (vs. 11-18) and stay alert. For the bible clearly reminds us, not to be conformed to this world, but we transformed by the renewing of your mind (Romans 12:2)

A Trigger Plan of Action

Developing a strategy to triumph over your triggers is helpful. Therefore, when you find yourself prompted or irritated in some way, shape, or form; it's always good to have a game plan. This can help you notice patterns and possible triggers.

Remember to:

⇨ Recognize your triggers to better manage them

⇨ Replace them with positive thoughts and actions

⇨ Recite the Word to help you overcome

Learn a few things to avoid that can cause a trigger, such as:

⇨self-medicating to cope or take the edge of your pain (such as using drugs or drinking)

⇨risky situations like events, birthday parties or hostile environments that may trigger a response from you

⇨negative thinking patterns such as denial (I can control it), rationalizing (one will not hurt), entitlement (I deserve it), sabotage (I don't care), justifying (how else will I deal with my stress)

Take a moment now and make a list of people, places or things that you need to avoid to maintain your focus.

_____

_____

_____

_____

_____

_____

You may also begin journaling your thoughts, feelings or experiences. This can be therapeutic or helpful to write out things you are grateful for or make you happy. But take note when something has made you emotional, so that you can better learn what your triggers are. This can help normalize your experiences and help you look after yourself as best as you can. Lastly, consider doing breathing techniques or exercises that can assist you with your anxiety or emotions as a way of managing your triggers.

Remember, as you triumph over your triggers by following the Lord, know that God always causes you to Triumph!
(2 Corinthians 2:14a)

A PERSONAL PLEDGE OF COMMITMENT

This document serves as a declaration to you choosing to fully embrace and walk in your freedom. In this place, you make a personal pledge of commitment and accept your rightful position.

"Father, I _____ *, surrender my all to you this day; so that I may experience a sense of liberty. Therefore, I confess and release every hurt, doubt, rejection, pain, abuse, and unforgiveness from my past. I affirm all of who I am; all that I was created to be, and all that You have purposed for me to do; as I have now made the commitment to Triumph Through My Pain. I am a Champion."*

_____

Signature

On this _____ day of _____, 20___ of our Lord Jesus Christ; a commitment has been filed for ownership into the bridal chamber by the blood of Jesus shed for all humanity. There is an inauguration of the Old Covenant transferred into the New covenant by bloodshed once and for all. *"Indeed, under the law almost everything is purified with blood, and without the shedding of blood there is no forgiveness of sins"* (Hebrews 9:22).

References

Wright, Lorraine. LCSW-R *"Gatehouse Professional Center,"* Private Practice, Lockport New York, wrightglte1@gmail.com.

Kessler, David, "Finding Meaning: *The Six Stage of Gri*ef," Published by Simon and Schuster, September 2020.

Elliott, Charlotte, (18 March 1789 – 22 September 1871) was an English poet, hymn writer, and editor. She is best known by two hymns, *"Just As I Am"*.

Yeates, Nicole, *"What are the Three Behavioural Triggers,"* Peak Performance Speaker, August 2021, https://www.linkedin.com/pulse/what-three-behavioural-triggers-nicole-yeates

Bakersfield Behavioral Healthcare Hospital, *"6 Tips for Overcoming Negative Thinking,"* October 2019 https://www.bakersfieldbehavioral.com/blog/overcoming-negative-thinking

The Loss Foundation. UK National Charity, *"Triggers in Grief,"* 2011 - 2023 https://thelossfoundation.org/triggers-in-grief/

Nova Recovery Center, Avoiding High Risk Situations. https://novarecoverycenter.com/treatment-programs/avoid-high-risk-situations/

RESOURCES AND HELPFUL TOOLS

Duncan, Ligon, "When Pain Is Real and God Seems Silent: Finding Hope in the Psalms," 2020.

Elliot, Elizabeth, *Suffering Is Never for Nothing*," February 1, 2019.

Guthrie, Nance, Holding On to Hope: "*A Pathway through Suffering to the Heart of God,*" December 16, 2015

Kessler, David, Because Love Never Dies: "*Finding the meaning of grief through the Five Stage of Dying, with Free Access to Healing the Five Areas of Grief Video,*" *pertaining to* Elizabeth Kubler – *Ross, MD,* Grief.com

Kessler, David, "*Tender Hearts,*" https://www.davidkesslertraining.com, "Grief: Releasing Pain, Remembering Love & Finding Meaning," https://www.facebook.com Facebook Groups.

Langberg, Diane, "Redeeming Power, Understanding Authority and Abuse in the Church," October 2020.

Richards, James B., *"How to Stop the Pain,"* December 2001.

Trauma Research. https://integratedlistening.com/what-is-trauma/, 2020.

Schauer, Maggie and Elbert, Thomas. 2015. Dissociation Following Traumatic Stress. Zeitschrift für Psychologie / Journal of Psychology 218, NO. 2 (February). https://doi.org/10.1027/0044-3409/a000018.

U.S. Department of Veterans Affairs. PTSD: National Center for PTSD. How Common Is PTSD in Adults? https://www.ptsd.va.gov/understand/common/common_adults.asp

The Gateway Foundation. Common relapse triggers, https://gatewayfoundation.org

Acknowledgements

Although this period of my life was filled with uncertainty in drafting this book, I thank Ms. Dawn Nicole McMillan, Madame Publisher; my Publisher and Chief- Editor who was willing to take on this dreamer who was conquering treatments of Chemotherapy and Radiation for Breast Cancer. She heard and saw me; then launched this book to where it is. She pushed through with great wisdom, clarity of hearing from the heart of the Father and allowing Him to download as this writer came into agreement. This reset in my life was welcomed because it pushed me forward in birthing forth my dream seed:

When Tears Become Blood - Triumph through Pain.

An incredibly special thanks to my Co-Editor, Rachel Henderson for her insight of building a house from one brick into a mansion. She allowed this writer to rise through the ashes into something beautiful in sharing the gift of this book.

In addition, this would not have been made possible without the encouragement and support of all my beloved children and dear friends.

Therefore, I thank you All for the love, your gifts and your heart's contribution.

Lady Dianna

About The Author
DIANNA HENDERSON

Dianna Henderson served in ministry with her late husband Bishop William Henderson for over 35 years and leads with a team; The Light of the World Mission Inc. As a leader, she shares her giftings as a bridge builder, collaborator in ministry, mentor, youth activist, professional social worker, transformational leader, and political activist who honorably served in the United States Army. She has held numerous leadership conferences and seminars based on her self-published books, *"Releasing the Champion Inside and Uncovering the Treasure Within,"* and *"Dancing in the Secret Chambers."* She hosted her own radio program, *Matters of the Heart,* inspirational television program, *Mega SEED,* as well as producing an independent documentary, *Hues of Humanity Let's Begin the Conversation,* with daughter Rachel Henderson. In recognition of her service, she was a recipient of the Congressional Award, Celebration of Excellence Award, the Army Commendation Medal of Meritorious Service, Community Service Award, Commander's Award of Leadership, Proclamations, and numerous other honors. Yet, Dianna praises God for all His Mighty Acts!

For inquiries, special request or booking information, please contact Dianna at:

(716) 393-5040

Champions@mail.com

Championslevelup.com

Champions Level Up (author)

Champions Level Up Author

54019281R00071